For Bruce and Myron,
without whose encouragement
this book wouldn't be.

—Lv/dL

Published by Sunbird Books, an imprint of Phoenix International Publications, Inc.

8501 West Higgins Road   34 Seymour Street   Heimhuder Straße 81
Chicago, Illinois 60631   London W1H 7JE   20148 Hamburg

www.sunbirdkidsbooks.com

Text © 2023 Laurel van der Linde
Illustrations © 2023 Phoenix International Publications, Inc.

Library of Congress Control Number: 2022933861

ISBN: 978-1-5037-6409-5 Printed in China

Black Swans

Written by Laurel van der Linde
Illustrated by Sawyer Cloud

sunbird books

ESSIE MARIE DORSEY

1893–1967

When she clicked her castanets and danced the flamenco, everyone thought she was Spanish. **ESSIE MARIE DORSEY** didn't correct them. In the 1920s, she knew the only way she could enter the white world of American ballet was to hide her Black heritage.

In New York City, Essie Marie studied with Russians Mikhail Mordkin and Mikhail Fokine, who had choreographed dances for the famous Ballets Russes. She joined Mordkin's troupe but was never a full member, and she performed only Spanish dances, not ballet.

Still she danced...

If Essie Marie couldn't be a ballet dancer, she would make sure others could.

Back then, Black children were not allowed to dance with white children. So in 1926, she opened the Essie Marie Dorsey School of Dancing in Philadelphia. She went door-to-door asking Black parents to send their children to her school...and they did!

ARTHUR MITCHELL
1934–2018

Dancing with a hat and cane, **ARTHUR MITCHELL** auditioned for the High School of Performing Arts. His dream was to dance on Broadway. But Broadway wasn't hiring Black dancers.

So Arthur started to study ballet. He thought if he became a good ballet dancer, Broadway couldn't turn him down. He became so skilled at ballet that, in the early 1950s, the School of American Ballet awarded him a scholarship. There, his talent caught the eye of George Balanchine, the artistic director of New York City Ballet, and Arthur was invited to join the company. He was their only Black dancer.

Arthur worked hard to perfect the jumps, turns, and beats of classical ballet. His work was noticed, and he was promoted—becoming the first Black principal dancer of New York City Ballet.

But when he was partnered with Diana Adams in Balanchine's new ballet, *Agon*, the audience was shocked. A Black man dancing with a white woman was not accepted in 1957. The crowd jeered and booed.

Still he danced...

After twelve successful years dancing with New York City Ballet, Arthur wanted to do more for the Black community. In 1969, in the midst of the Civil Rights Movement, Arthur used $25,000 of his own money to cofound Dance Theatre of Harlem. This ballet company and school for Black dancers continues Arthur's work to this day.

CHRISTIAN HOLDER

1949–

CHRISTIAN HOLDER was only four years old when he danced for the Queen! Born in the Crown Colony of Trinidad, he joined his father's dance company at a young age. Boscoe Holder and His Caribbean Dancers performed at the coronation of Queen Elizabeth II. The family moved to England, and Christian began ballet lessons at age seven. In 1963, when Christian was fourteen, the famous modern dancer Martha Graham offered him a scholarship to study with her company in New York City.

In New York, Christian attended the High School of Performing Arts. There, choreographer Robert Joffrey saw him dance and invited him to join The Joffrey Ballet.

Soon, Christian was dancing principal roles. But when he was assigned the lead in a new ballet called *Astarte*, the principal ballerina's husband refused to have her partnered by a Black man.

Still he danced...

The ballerina was replaced, and Christian danced the leading role. *Astarte* became a signature work of The Joffrey Ballet in the 1970s.

After dancing with the Joffrey for seventeen years, Christian left to work with San Francisco Opera as a guest soloist and choreographer.

Later, he returned to the Joffrey for a memorable performance as one of the Stepsisters in *Cinderella*.

DWIGHT RHODEN

1962–

He had no formal training, but **DWIGHT RHODEN** loved to make up dances and compete in school dance contests. After graduating high school, he began ballet classes and studied with the Dayton Contemporary Dance Company in Ohio. Next, he joined Les Ballets Jazz de Montréal, where he was the only Black dancer in the company. After much hard work and three auditions, he was invited to join Alvin Ailey American Dance Theatre.

Long and lean, Dwight worked hard to keep up with the other men in the company, who were more muscular. The more he danced, the more he fell in love with making up his own dances. Dwight sent samples of his choreography to ballet companies. None responded.

Still he danced...

Slowly, Dwight realized it wasn't the quality of his work that was holding

him back—it was the color of his skin.

He would have to work harder than other choreographers for his work

to be accepted, and so he did. Finally, Pittsburgh Ballet Theatre asked Dwight

to stage a piece. Soon, the directors of other companies wanted his work.

In 1994, he partnered with dancer Desmond Richardson to cofound

Complexions Contemporary Ballet. The company continues to bring innovative

and inclusive dance to countries around the world.

MISTY COPELAND

1982–

MISTY COPELAND had never thought of being a ballet dancer, but her drill team teacher thought she should try it. So at age thirteen, Misty took her very first lesson in the school gym, wearing her gym clothes!

She was a natural. After three months, she was dancing *en pointe*.

When she was seventeen, Misty auditioned for American Ballet Theatre and was accepted into the Studio Company. Two years later, she joined the corps de ballet in the main company.

It wasn't easy being the only Black dancer. During rehearsals of *Swan Lake*, Misty was pulled from the "Dance of the Little Swans" at the last minute—because the color of her skin didn't match the other ballerinas.

Still she danced...

In 2011, music superstar Prince invited Misty to dance in his show at Madison Square Garden in New York City. She had already been a soloist with American Ballet Theatre for four years, but now her career took flight. She was cast in the title role of ABT's new production of *The Firebird*.

Misty knew how important this performance was for her career, and for the Black community. But she got injured in rehearsal, and on her opening night she danced on a fractured leg.

After her leg healed, she returned to ABT and kept earning big, important roles. She was promoted to Principal Dancer in 2015, the first Black ballerina to achieve that title in ABT's history.

MICHAELA DePRINCE

1995–

She was the least-favored child in her orphanage in Sierra Leone, where the children were given numbers instead of names. Her dark skin had white spots, a condition called vitiligo. She watched as other orphans were adopted. Nobody wanted a spotted child.

One day, the wind lodged a magazine in the gate of the orphanage. On the cover was a picture of a ballerina. Though she had never seen a ballerina, the four-year-old knew that this was what she wanted to be.

An American family adopted her and gave her their family name. MICHAELA DePRINCE flew from West Africa to her new home in New Jersey, where she started ballet lessons.

At age eight, Michaela danced in Pennsylvania Ballet's production of *The Nutcracker*.

At fifteen, she competed in the 2010 Youth America Grand Prix, the largest competition

for ballet students in the world. She won a full scholarship to the Jacqueline Kennedy Onassis

School at American Ballet Theatre.

When Michaela was eighteen, Dance Theatre of Harlem offered her a contract. She had

become a beautiful Black Swan.

But Michaela dreamed of dancing with a traditional company.
In 2013, she auditioned for and was invited to join Dutch National Ballet
in the Netherlands. She quickly rose through the ranks, from apprentice
to corps de ballet to the starring role of Swan in that company's new
production of *Coppélia*.

In 2021, she returned to the United States to join Boston Ballet.

Still she dances...

...and you can too!

Author's Note

The desire to dance is born in you. It is a gift which evolves into a passion that demands to be fulfilled. To have that passion thwarted is an injustice. Dancing is not an easy life—but the chance to answer the call of one's soul and defy the bonds of physicality and gravity should never be denied.

There are many more Black Swans—more than can fit in the pages of this book—whose daring acts of dance paved the way for others to follow in their footsteps. Here are but a few:

Janet Collins (1917–2003), Principal Dancer, Metropolitan Opera Ballet

Raven Wilkinson (1935–2018), Soloist, Dutch National Ballet

Virginia Johnson (1950–), Principal Dancer, Dance Theatre of Harlem

Mel A. Tomlinson (1954–2019), Principal Dancer, New York City Ballet

Desmond Richardson (1969–), Principal Dancer, American Ballet Theatre

Carlos Acosta (1973–), Principal Dancer, Royal Ballet

Aesha Ash (1977–), Principal Dancer, New York City Ballet

Calvin Royal III (1988–), Principal Dancer, American Ballet Theatre

Author **Laurel van der Linde** began ballet class at age four. At seventeen, she toured with Oukhtomsky Ballet Classique and Los Angeles Ballet. She loved dancing *en pointe*, but her feet did not. So she traded her pointe shoes for character heels and danced on Broadway in *My Fair Lady, A Chorus Line, Seven Brides for Seven Brothers*, and Gower Champion's *Annie Get Your Gun*. Now she teaches creative writing at the University of California, Los Angeles.

Illustrator **Sawyer Cloud** is a self-taught artist from Madagascar. She still lives on her native island, along with her family and her two pets. She loves sunny days, singing, and sharing stories with the world.